Max and the drum

Written by Nicola Moon

Illustrated by Kay Widdowson

Max was a little brown mouse.
Pecky was a big black crow.
One day Max and Pecky went
to the market.

Some clowns went down the street.
'Boom! Boom! Boom!' went the drum.
'Toot! Toot! Toot!' went the trumpet.

'I want to play the trumpet,'
said Pecky.
'I want to play the drum,'
said Max.

The clowns saw some children.
They put down the drum and
the trumpet.

'Now I can play the trumpet,'
said Pecky.
'No, you can't,' said Max.
'Yes, I can,' said Pecky.

Pecky blew and blew and blew.
But she could not play the trumpet.

'I can play the drum,' said Max.

'No, you can't,' said Pecky.

'Yes, I can,' said Max.

Max jumped on the drum.

He jumped up and he jumped down.

'I can play the drum,' he said.

Max went up and up and up.
He went into the tree.

'Help,' said Max.
'I can't get down.'
'I will help you,' said Pecky.

'Get on my back,' said Pecky.
And down they went.